THE GROSS LIFE CYCLE

OF A HIPPOPOTAMUS

BookLife
PUBLISHING

©2022
BookLife Publishing Ltd.
King's Lynn
Norfolk PE30 4LS

ISBN: 978-1-80155-124-3

Written by:
William Anthony

Edited by:
Emilie Dufresne

Designed by:
Amy Li

BookLife
freedom
Readers

PHOTO CREDITS

Images are courtesy of Shutterstock.com. With thanks to Getty Images, Thinkstock Photo and iStockphoto.

Recurring images – Milan M (grunge shapes), Sonechko57 (splat shapes), Jojje, Infinity32829 (paper background), Rimma Z (watercolour splatters), Sopelkin, Ermak Oksana (decorative vectors). Cover – Eric Isslee, p1 – Eric Isslee, mijatmijatovic, Natasha Pankina, p2–3 – Eric Isslee, Jody, p4–5 – Flashon Studio, Krakenimages.com, kurhan, zulufoto, p6–7 – Nils Versemann, Dmitry Balakirev, p8–9 – EcoPrint, Stu Porter, p10–11 – Ondrej Prosicky, PhotocechCZ, p12–13 – Mogens Trolle, Graeme Shannon, p14–15 – LesPalenik, wk1003mike, Gilmanshin, p16–17 – Daniela Schroeder, Phillip Allaway, p18–19 – BigBoom, OPgrapher, nikiteev, p20–21 – Stu Porter, Henk Bentlage, p22–23 – COLOMBO NICOLA, Stu Porter, Big Boom, EcoPrint

HIPPOPOTAMUS
CONTENTS

Page 4   **What Is a Life Cycle?**

Page 5   **Gross Life Cycles**

Page 6   **What Is a Hippopotamus?**

Page 8   **Calves and Cows**

Page 10   **Bulls**

Page 12   **Fight for the Right**

Page 14   **Hippo-Hippo-Hooray!**

Page 16   **Good Things Come to an End**

Page 18   **A Gross Life**

Page 22   **Gross Life Cycle of a Hippopotamus**

Page 23   **Get Exploring!**

Page 24   **Questions**

WHAT IS A LIFE CYCLE?

All animals, plants and humans go through different stages of their life as they grow and change. This is called a life cycle.

Baby ➤ **Child** ➤ **Adult**

GROSS LIFE CYCLES

Not all life cycles are the same. They can be quick or slow. They can have lots of steps or very few. Worst of all, they can be sloppy, ploppy, full of splashes and splats and be absolutely gross!

WHAT IS A HIPPOPOTAMUS?

The hippopotamus, or hippo, is a type of mammal. This means that it has warm blood, a backbone and makes milk for its babies. Hippos can normally be found near rivers or lakes in Africa.

Hippos have a disgusting, gross life cycle. There are a lot of smells, splats and slops. It is not a nice sight!

CALVES AND COWS

Female adult hippos are called cows. Cows are pregnant for around eight months before they give birth. Cows usually give birth to just one baby hippo.

Baby hippos are called calves. Calves live on land and under water. Calves can close their ears and noses when they are in water, just like their parents.

Cow

Calf

9

BULLS

Male adult hippos are called bulls. Bulls usually stick to one part of a river. This part of the river is where they will mate with female hippos.

There is usually one male in a group of hippos who will mate with the females. This male protects his territory and the female hippos in some very gross ways.

FIGHT FOR THE RIGHT

If a new bull tries to take over another bull's territory, they may fight. The winner of the fight will then be the only bull that can mate there.

When a bull really wants to mark out his territory, he does something absolutely gross. He does a big poo and then sprays it everywhere by quickly flicking his tail.

HIPPO-HIPPO HOORAY!

When the time is right, female hippos will come to the river to mate. But to impress a female, the bull does something very disgusting...

The bull flicks his poo absolutely everywhere. If a cow likes the bull's poo shower, she may poo near him too. She will then mate with him.

GOOD THINGS COME TO AN END

Eight months later, the pregnant cow will give birth to a calf. The calf will grow up into a bull or a cow and the life cycle will start again.

Eventually the adult hippo will die. Hippos normally live up to the age of 40 in the wild.

A GROSS LIFE

Hippos live very gross lives. When they mark out their territory, they leave smelly signposts for other hippos. The signposts are made of poo.

In fact, hippo poo can be deadly. Hippos can poo so much that fish can die from it. When there is too much hippo poo in the river, bad chemicals build up and make it hard for the fish to breathe.

Do you sweat when it's hot outside? Hippos do, too. Hippo sweat is red and it protects the hippo from the sun. It works just like sun cream does on you.

Hippos make all sorts of gross noises. They grunt, snort and sniffle. Some hippo noises can be as loud as a rock concert!

GROSS LIFE CYCLE OF A HIPPOPOTAMUS

1 A cow gives birth to a calf.

2 The calf grows into an adult bull or cow.

3 The adult uses poo to attract another hippo.

4 The bull and the cow will mate.

GET EXPLORING!

Have you ever seen a hippo? Many zoos keep hippos that you can look at. Find out if there is a zoo near you that you can visit!

QUESTIONS

1 What age do hippos normally live up to in the wild?

2 What continent can hippos be found on?
a) Europe
b) South America
c) Africa

3 What are baby hippos called?

4 How do bulls mark out their territory?

5 Have you ever seen a hippo? If you haven't, would you like to?